Contents

KU-016-002

	The People in This Story	4
1	A Strange Story	5
2	Aziz Gets a Job	12
3	Flamingo Park	20
4	A Mysterious Journey	28
5	Plans for a Kidnap	36
6	Kidnap!	44
7	Rescue	53
	Points for Understanding	62

This story takes place in London and in the south-west of Britain. Britain is divided into areas which are called 'counties'. Cornwall and Devon are two counties in the south-west of Britain.

The People in This Story

Aziz

Sheila

Tom

Brody

Mrs Dempster

Bill

Dave Morris

Jim Wood

Prince Khalifa

1

A Strange Story

Aziz Abdalla was a student in London. He was a student from an Arab country. Aziz was studying engineering at Farraday College. He was nineteen years old and he was in his first year at the college.

Aziz was a cheerful and lively young man and he was always making jokes. But he worked hard and his teachers were very pleased with him. All the other students at the college liked him.

All the students liked Aziz, and lots of them were his friends. At weekends and during holidays, Aziz visited many interesting places in London. He visited these places with his friends.

Aziz visited many interesting places in London with his friends.

All the students at Farraday College had to take examinations in June, at the end of the college year. After that, the long summer holidays began.

The students' last examination was on the afternoon of the last Thursday in June. After the examination ended, Aziz went to the students' club with two of his friends, Tom and Sheila. Like Aziz, Tom was studying engineering. Sheila was studying tourism.

The three friends bought cups of coffee. Then Tom and Sheila told Aziz about their plans for the long summer holidays – the months of July, August and September.

'We're going to Cornwall,' said Tom. 'We're going to work there for the summer months. We're going to travel to Cornwall tomorrow morning.'

'Cornwall?' said Aziz. 'Where's that?'

'It's in the south-west of England,' replied Sheila. 'Look – I've got a map here. I'll show you Cornwall on the map.'

Sheila took a map from her bag and she opened it out on the table in front of them.

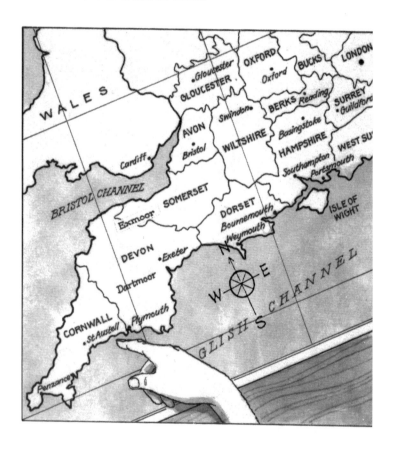

'We've both got jobs in Cornwall for the summer holidays,' Tom told Aziz. 'We're both going to work in a holiday camp. It's called Flamingo Park.'

Sheila took something else from her bag. 'Here's a brochure for the camp,' she said.

Aziz looked at the brochure.

**FLAMINGO PARK HOLIDAY CAMP
NEAR HELSTON – CORNWALL**

**FUN AND GAMES FOR ALL THE FAMILY
AMAZING VIEWS OVER CLIFFS AND BEACHES
TO THE ATLANTIC OCEAN**

- excellent accommodation in tents or luxury caravans
- staff to take care of children
- top quality food in family restaurant
- superb shopping facilities
- well-equipped games rooms
- children's playground and paddling pool

**COME AND JOIN US!
ENJOY A CAREFREE HOLIDAY!**

For details write to:
Flamingo Park Holiday Camp
near Helston
Cornwall

'There's a restaurant at the camp,' Tom said. 'I've got a job as a waiter there.'

'And I'm going to help with the children,' said Sheila.

'What are *you* going to do during the summer holidays, Aziz?' Sheila asked.

'I'm going to stay here in London,' replied Aziz. 'I don't have enough money to fly back home. And I don't have enough money for a holiday.'

'Why don't you try to get a job?' Tom asked Aziz.

'Perhaps there will be a job for Aziz at Flamingo Park,' said Sheila. 'We'll ask the manager about it when we get there.'

'Yes. But wait a moment,' Tom said excitedly. 'I remember something! Aziz, let's look at the notice-board in the corridor.'

Aziz went into the corridor with Tom and Sheila. They stood in front of the notice-board.

'Yes! There it is, Aziz,' said Tom. He pointed to an advertisement on the notice-board.

'What good luck, Aziz!' said Tom. 'You must phone that number. This ad looks interesting!'

'Wait a moment,' said Sheila. 'I'm not sure about that ad. I saw the person who put the ad on the notice-board. It was a man. I didn't like him. He looked dangerous. He might be a criminal. Be careful, Aziz!'

The three friends talked for a few more minutes. Then Aziz said goodbye to Tom and Sheila. Tom wrote an address on a piece of paper and he gave it to Aziz.

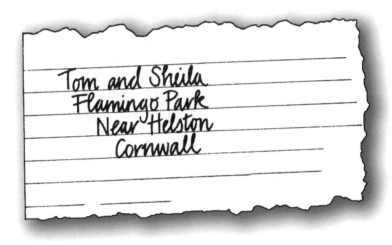

Tom and Sheila
Flamingo Park
Near Helston
Cornwall

'This is our address at Flamingo Park,' he said. 'If there is a job for you there, we'll write and tell you. But remember to phone the number on that ad tomorrow morning. You might have a holiday – and you might be paid for it.'

'But please take care, Aziz,' said Sheila.

11

2

Aziz Gets a Job

On Friday morning, Aziz got up early. He went to a public phone box and he made a call. He called the number from the ad on the college notice-board.

A man answered the phone.

'Hello.'

'I'm phoning about the ad in the students' club at Farraday College,' said Aziz.

'Can you speak Arabic?' the man asked.

'Yes,' said Aziz. 'I am an Arab and I can speak Arabic.'

'That's very important,' said the man. 'How old are you?'

Aziz told him.

'Can you come for an interview this afternoon?'

'Yes,' said Aziz. 'My exams finished yesterday. I have no more classes.'

'Come at two o'clock,' said the man. 'This is the address.'

The man gave Aziz an address in central London. Aziz wrote down the address carefully.

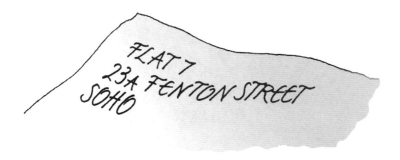

FLAT 7
23A FENTON STREET
SOHO

'My name is Aziz Abdalla,' said Aziz. 'What's your name?'

But there was no answer. The man had put down his phone.

Aziz was hopeful. 'Perhaps I'll get the job,' he thought. 'Then I'll write to Tom and Sheila. What a surprise it will be for them!'

Aziz took a street map of London from his pocket. He studied the map carefully and he found Fenton Street. Fenton Street was not far from Leicester Square station on the Underground.

Aziz arrived at Leicester Square Underground station at two o'clock in the afternoon. He walked to Fenton Street.

Fenton Street was narrow and dirty. Above a dark doorway, Aziz saw the number 23A. He went into the building and climbed some steep, narrow stairs. Flat 7 was at the top of the building.

Aziz knocked at the door of Flat 7. He heard a woman's voice.

'Come in, please. The door isn't locked,' she said.

Aziz pushed the door open and walked into a small room. There were two people in the room – a woman and a man. They were both about thirty years old.

Aziz was surprised. The room did not look like an office. Aziz saw a small desk and some broken shelves. But there was no typewriter and there was no telephone.

The woman was sitting on a chair behind the small desk. The man was sitting on another chair at the side of the desk. There was a third chair in front of the desk.

'Sit down, please,' said the woman.

Aziz sat on the third chair. For a few moments, there was silence in the room. The man and the woman looked at Aziz very carefully.

'What's your name?' asked the woman.

'Aziz Abdalla,' Aziz replied.

'I'm Mrs Dempster,' said the woman. 'And this is Mr Brody. We want to ask you a few questions.'

They both looked at Aziz and smiled. But Aziz did not feel comfortable. Mr Brody had a hard, cruel face.

'Tell me about your family,' said Brody. 'Are they living with you here in London?'

'No,' replied Aziz. 'I am here alone.'

'Do you have lots of friends?' Mrs Dempster asked.

'Yes, of course,' replied Aziz. 'I've lots of friends at college. But our examinations finished yesterday and all my friends have gone away. Some have gone home and others have got jobs for the summer holidays.'

Mrs Dempster looked at Brody. He nodded at her.

'And you are looking for a job too, Aziz,' said Mrs Dempster. 'Do you want this job?'

Aziz thought for a few moments. 'Will you tell me more about it?' he asked.

'You will be a companion to a young prince from an Arab country,' said Brody. 'Everything will be paid for – your food and your accommodation. You will have this job for six weeks.'

'How much will I be paid?' asked Aziz.

'We will pay you one thousand pounds,' Brody replied.

'If you take this job,' said Mrs Dempster, 'you mustn't tell anyone about it. We don't want the Prince's enemies to know about his visit to England.'

'Now tell us,' said Brody, 'do you want the job?'

Aziz did not reply. There was silence in the room. Brody and Dempster sat quietly and looked at Aziz. Aziz did not feel happy. There was something strange about the room. And there was something strange about Brody. Was he a criminal?

Brody repeated the question. 'Do you want the job, Aziz. We have to know now.'

The young man thought for a few more seconds. One thousand pounds was a lot of money. And the job – being a companion to an Arab prince – would not be difficult. Aziz decided to take the job.

'Yes,' he replied. 'I want the job.'

'Very good,' said Brody.

'Can you leave London this evening?' asked Mrs Dempster.

'Yes,' replied Aziz.

Mrs Dempster smiled coldly.

'You will find your instructions and eighty pounds in this envelope,' she said. 'Goodbye, Aziz.'

———

When they were alone, Brody turned to Mrs Dempster.

'Well done,' he said, laughing. 'Writing that ad was your idea, and it worked.'

'Yes,' agreed Mrs Dempster. 'It was a good idea to advertise for an Arab student. This boy is the same age as the Prince. If we put the Prince's clothes on him, he will look like the Prince.'

'Good! Now we must give Bill his instructions for tonight,' said Brody. 'And then we must drive to the house in Cornwall as quickly as possible.'

3

Flamingo Park

On Friday morning, while Aziz was looking for a job, Tom and Sheila were standing at the side of a busy road. Tom was holding up a piece of card with CORNWALL written on it.

Tom and Sheila were trying to get to Cornwall. They did not have much money, so they were hitch-hiking. They were asking drivers to give them a lift. They were asking drivers to take them to Cornwall for nothing.

The young people waited and waited. But nobody was going to Cornwall. Tom and Sheila had to wait for two hours. But at last, a small van stopped.

'You want to go to Cornwall,' said the young man who was driving the van. 'I'm going there. Get in!'

Tom and Sheila climbed into the back of the van. They were very uncomfortable, but that did not worry them. They were on their way to Cornwall!

After an hour, the driver stopped at the motorway service area at Membury.

Tom and Sheila were pleased when the van stopped at the service area. They went into the coffee shop with the driver.

'My name's John,' the van driver told them. 'I'm a student at Cambridge University. Are you both students?'

'Yes, were are,' Tom replied. 'I'm Tom. And this is Sheila. We're both students at Farraday College in London.'

'I'm on my way to Cornwall,' John told them. 'But, today, I have to visit some friends in Devon. They live in Exeter. I'm going to drive on to Cornwall tomorrow.'

'We won't get to Exeter until this evening,' John went on. 'If you stay in Exeter tonight, I'll take you on to Cornwall in the morning.'

'That's a good idea,' said Sheila. 'But where will we stay in Exeter?'

'Have you got tents?' John asked.

'Yes, we've got tents,' Tom replied.

'Good,' said John. 'My friends have a large garden. You can put up your tents in their garden.'

'Where are you going to in Cornwall?' asked Tom.

'I'm going to visit some friends in a small town called Helston,' replied John.

'Oh, that's great, John!' said Tom. 'We're going to Flamingo Park. It's near Helston.'

———

Tom and Sheila stayed the night with John's friends in Exeter. The next morning, the three of them went on to Cornwall. John took them all the way to Flamingo Park. They got there before twelve o'clock.

'Thank you very much, John,' Sheila said. 'You've helped us a lot. You must come and have a meal with us one evening.'

'Thank you for the invitation,' said John. 'I'm going to stay with my friends in Helston for a week. Their phone number is Helston 4321. Call me soon.'

A moment later, Tom and Sheila were standing at the entrance to Flamingo Park. They were on a high hill and they could see the sea below them.

'That's the Atlantic Ocean,' Sheila said to Tom. 'Isn't it beautiful?'

Flamingo Park was on the side of the hill. At the bottom of the hill, there was a steep cliff. Below the cliff, there was a long, sandy beach beside the sea.

There were many caravans and tents on the hill-side. Flamingo Park was a holiday camp. The holidaymakers stayed in the caravans and tents.

The two students walked down the hill, towards the entrance to the camp.

At the entrance to the holiday camp, were a shop and a restaurant. There was also a building for indoor games. The holidaymakers went there in the evenings or when the weather was bad. Behind this building, there was an amusement area for children – the Fun Fair. It had swings and roundabouts and a tiny railway. There was also a paddling pool.

A man came out of a door marked RECEPTION, and walked towards them. He was smiling and he looked very friendly.

'Hello,' he said. 'My name is Dave Morris. I'm the manager here. Are you Tom and Sheila?'

'Yes,' replied Tom. 'It's lovely here, Mr Morris.'

'Call me Dave,' said Mr Morris. 'I'll take you to your rooms. Your work starts on Monday. You're free this weekend.'

'Well, I'd like to see an old tin mine,' said Tom. 'There are lots of old mines in Cornwall. I'm studying engineering and I'm interested in mines.'

'There's an old tin mine here, below the cliff,' said Dave. 'The entrance is in the side of the cliff. You can see the entrance from the beach.'

'Is the mine safe?' Sheila asked.

'No, it isn't,' replied Dave. 'It's very dangerous. We tell all the holidaymakers to keep away from the mine. So take care!'

'We'll be careful,' said Tom.

'Now I'll take you to your rooms,' said Dave. 'You can rest after your long journey. Lunch is at one o'clock.'

After lunch, Tom and Sheila walked down to the beach. The sun was shining. It was a beautiful afternoon.

Tom ran down to the edge of the water.

'What a marvellous place for swimming!' he shouted to Sheila. 'We can come here in our free time.'

The two friends sat on the sand and watched the waves.

'We forgot to ask Dave about a job for Aziz,' said Sheila. 'We must do that when we see him this evening.'

'Yes,' agreed Tom. 'I'm sure Aziz would like to be here with us.'

'Look!' said Sheila, pointing towards the cliff. 'There's the entrance to the old tin mine.'

'Let's go and look,' said Tom.

27

4

A Mysterious Journey

On Friday afternoon, Aziz packed some clothes into a small suitcase. He read his instructions again.

Aziz was not very happy. He was worried about this holiday job. The instructions were very strange and mysterious.

Be at platform 14
on Euston Station
tonight at 10.30.
A man called Bill
will meet you there.

Aziz thought about Mr Brody. The man's face had looked hard and tough. Was he a criminal? And the instructions told Aziz to meet a man called Bill. Who was Bill? Was *he* a criminal?

'What shall I do?' Aziz asked himself. 'If I ask Tom and Sheila, they will give me advice. They will tell me what to do. But I can't speak to them today. They are travelling to Cornwall.'

Then Aziz thought about the thousand pounds. One thousand pounds was a lot of money. He decided to go to Euston Station.

Aziz arrived at Euston Station at ten o'clock. He stood near the entrance to Platform 14, and he waited. He did not feel happy.

A train was going to leave Platform 14 at eleven o'clock. The train was going to Glasgow.

'Glasgow is in Scotland,' Aziz thought. 'Perhaps I am going to work in Scotland. That will be interesting.'

Aziz waited until a quarter to eleven. The entrance to Platform 14 was now crowded with passengers who were going to Glasgow.

Then a man came up and stood beside him.

'You're Aziz,' he said quietly. 'And I'm Bill. Come with me.'

Aziz walked towards Platform 14.

'No! Not that way!' the man said roughly. 'This way. Follow me!'

Aziz and Bill walked out of the station and they turned into a small, dark street. Bill stopped beside a large black car. He opened one of the car doors and told Aziz to get in.

Aziz stood on the pavement. He did not move. What was happening? Was he in danger? He had not told anyone about the meeting at Fenton Street. He had not told anyone about the job. He had not told anyone about the meeting at Euston Station. If there was any trouble, no one would help him. Aziz felt afraid.

'Where are we going?' he asked.

'You'll find out when we get there,' the rough man replied.

Aziz got into the car and Bill drove off.

Bill drove quickly through the streets of London. Aziz sat in the back of the car. He was silent and afraid.

Half an hour later, they were out of London and driving along a motorway. Soon, they came to a large sign. Aziz turned his head and read it quickly. They were on the M4 motorway.

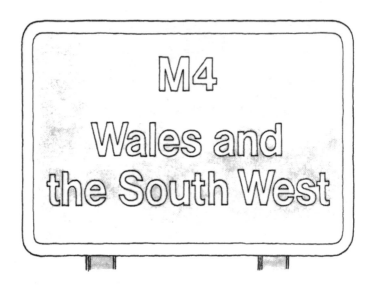

After about an hour, the car stopped at a motorway service area. Aziz saw a sign which said MEMBURY SERVICES.

'We're going to stop here for half an hour,' said Bill. 'You can have some coffee and something to eat. We have a long way to go.'

'But *where* are we going?' Aziz asked again.

'You'll find out when we get there,' said Bill.

Aziz followed Bill into the restaurant. Bill went up to the counter and bought some coffee and some cheese sandwiches.

It was now the middle of the night and the restaurant was nearly empty. There was no one there who could help Aziz. And if he asked anyone for help, what could he tell them? Mrs Dempster and Brody had offered him a job. The job was secret but Dempster and Brody had already paid him £80. Perhaps he was worried about nothing. Perhaps everything would be all right.

Bill and Aziz drank their coffee and ate their sandwiches. They did not speak. All the time, Bill was watching Aziz carefully.

Aziz and Bill got back into the car and continued their journey. Soon, Aziz began to feel very sleepy. He tried to stay awake.

'I've been drugged,' he thought. 'Bill has put something in my coffee to make me sleep.'

After a few minutes, Aziz fell asleep. As he slept, he began to dream. It was a terrible dream. He was running down a long, dark tunnel. He was shouting in Arabic, 'Help! Help! Get me out!'

———

Aziz woke up slowly. It was daylight. How long had he been asleep? The car had left the motorway. Bill was driving along a narrow country lane. After a few moments, the car stopped at a crossroads. Aziz saw a signpost at the crossroads.

Suddenly, Aziz was happy. He was in Cornwall. He was not far from Tom and Sheila. Perhaps he *could* get help if he was in trouble.

Soon, the car stopped again, in front of a large gate. Bill got out of the car and opened the gate. He drove the car through the gateway, and into a field. He got out again and closed the gate. Then he drove across the field and along a rough track into a thick wood.

The morning sun was shining, but it was dark in the wood. Aziz saw an old stone house among the trees. The house looked very mysterious. Bill drove towards it.

'There are no other houses near here,' Aziz thought. 'Am I going to be a companion to a prince who is staying here?'

The car stopped in front of the old house. Mrs Dempster and Brody were standing near the door. They were both smiling.

5

Plans for a Kidnap

Aziz and Bill followed Brody and Mrs Dempster into the mysterious old house.

'We have some breakfast for you,' Mrs Dempster said to Aziz. 'And you'll be tired after your long journey. You can sleep after breakfast.'

Aziz sat down with Bill at a wooden table. They were in a large, dirty kitchen. Mrs Dempster brought Aziz a plate of fried eggs and a cup of coffee. Aziz ate the eggs but he was afraid to drink the coffee.

'Perhaps it's drugged,' he thought. 'They want to make me fall asleep again.'

Soon, Dempster and Brody left the room. Bill started to read a newspaper. There was a dead plant in a pot on the table. While Bill was reading the newspaper, Aziz poured his coffee into the plant pot.

After a short time, Mrs Dempster came back into the kitchen.

'Have you had enough to eat?' she asked.

'Yes, thank you,' said Aziz.

'Ah, you've drunk your coffee,' she continued. 'That's good. Now I'll take you to your bedroom and you can sleep. Come with me.'

Mrs Dempster's words were not an invitation. They were an order!

Aziz followed Mrs Dempster up some steep stairs. The wooden steps were badly worn and some were broken. The woman opened a door and Aziz followed her into a small room.

'This is your bedroom,' she said. 'Mr Brody has brought up your suitcase. Sleep well!'

Mrs Dempster walked out of the bedroom and closed the door behind her. Aziz looked around him. There was only one small window in the room. And it had metal bars across it.

Aziz lay on the bed. His mind was full of questions. Why had they brought him to this old house? Where was the Prince?

Then he heard a noise by the door. Someone was standing outside. He lay quietly on the bed. Next, he heard footsteps going down the stairs.

Aziz listened. A few minutes later, he heard a voice. Someone was speaking. It was Mrs Dempster.

Aziz was able to hear Mrs Dempster's voice because it was coming through a hole in the floor. He got off the bed and knelt on the floor. Now he could hear the voice more clearly.

'The boy is asleep,' Mrs Dempster was saying. 'That coffee will make him sleep for a long time. Now we can plan the kidnap.'

'But why is the boy here?' Bill asked.

'I'll explain it to you in a moment,' said Mrs Dempster. 'Let's go into the kitchen and have some coffee.'

They went on talking, but Aziz was unable to hear what they were saying.

———

In the kitchen, Mrs Dempster and Brody explained the plan to Bill.

'We know about the Prince's travel plans,' said Mrs Dempster. 'He is going to travel by train. He will leave London tomorrow. He will come to Penzance, here in Cornwall.'

'And no one is going to travel with him,' said Brody. 'He will be alone.'

'The train from London stops once between Cambourne and Penzance,' Mrs Dempster went on. 'The train stops at the station at Hayle. Look, here's a map of western Cornwall.'

She spread out a map on the kitchen table.

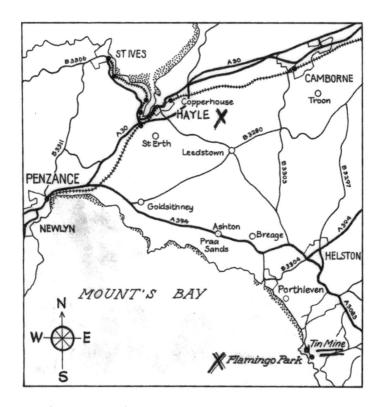

There was silence for a few moments. Then Bill spoke.

'Ah yes, I can see Hayle,' he said.

'There's a small station at Hayle,' said Mrs Dempster. 'And the express train from London stops there for a few minutes each evening. That's where we are going to kidnap Prince Khalifa.'

'Bill,' Mrs Dempster went on, 'you will drive to London early tomorrow morning. Get on the same train as the Prince. During the journey, talk to him. Be friendly to him. Then drug him! Make him go to sleep.'

'You mean – put something in his coffee?' asked Bill.

'That's right,' said Brody, laughing.

'When the train arrives at Hayle,' went on Mrs Dempster, 'we'll be waiting for you. We'll put Prince Khalifa into the car.'

'I don't understand,' said Bill. 'We can kidnap the Prince easily. We can take him from the train at Hayle. Then we can hide him in the tin mine until the ship arrives. Why do we need Aziz?'

'We need time, Bill,' replied Mrs Dempster. 'And Aziz will give us the time that we need.'

'But how?' asked Bill.

'We will tell Aziz, "Prince Khalifa is in danger,"' said Mrs Dempster. 'We will say, "Some evil people are planning to kidnap the Prince!" He will believe us.'

Brody and Bill laughed.

'That's good,' said Bill.

'It will be easy to trick Aziz,' the woman said. 'We will say, "The Prince is in great danger, Aziz. But you look like the Prince. And you can help the him." He will do what we tell him to do.'

'How would Aziz be helping Prince Khalifa?' asked Bill.

'He must pretend to be the Prince,' replied Mrs Dempster. 'We gave him the job because he looks like Prince Khalifa. He will take the place of the Prince when the train stops at Hayle.'

'But what will happen when the train gets to Penzance?' asked Bill.

'That's quite simple,' replied Mrs Dempster.

'When the train arrives in Penzance, a man will be

waiting for Prince Khalifa. The man is a friend of the Prince's father. But he is an Englishman. He has never met the Prince himself.'

'And then?' asked Bill.

'Then Aziz will tell the Englishman, "I am Prince Khalifa." And the man will believe him,' said Brody.

'And no one will know what has happened,' said Mrs Dempster. 'When someone does find out about the kidnapping, we will be on the ship. The Prince will be with us. Then we will demand two million pounds for his safe return.'

6

Kidnap!

When Mrs Dempster and Bill went into the kitchen, Aziz could no longer hear them. He sat on his bed again. He thought about what he *had* heard. He was worried.

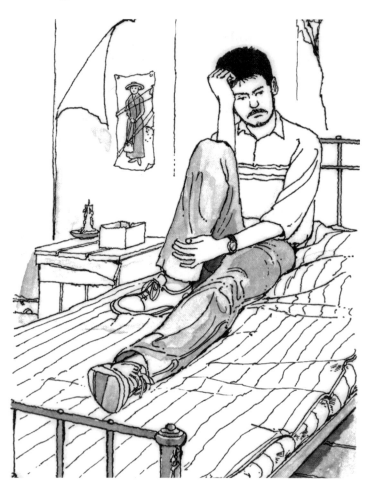

About two hours later, he heard someone coming up the stairs. He closed his eyes and he pretended to be asleep. The bedroom door opened and Mrs Dempster came into the room.

'Wake up,' she said to Aziz. 'It's time for lunch.'

Aziz opened his eyes. Mrs Dempster was smiling and she was trying to look friendly.

'When will I meet the Prince?' Aziz asked Mrs Dempster, as they went down the stairs.

'I'll tell you about that while we are having lunch,' she replied.

Brody and Bill were in the kitchen, sitting at the table. They both smiled at Aziz.

They were trying to look friendly. Aziz smiled at the two men. He had to pretend to be happy.

'Now, Aziz,' said Mrs Dempster, 'I'll tell you about Prince Khalifa.'

'The Prince's father has many enemies,' Mrs Dempster began. 'Some of them are planning to kidnap the Prince.'

'How terrible!' said Aziz.

'These enemies are planning to kidnap the Prince at Penzance —'

'Where's Penzance?' interrupted Aziz. 'And where are we now?'

'Penzance is in Cornwall. And we are in Cornwall now,' Mrs Dempster explained.

'Cornwall?' said Aziz. He pretended to be surprised. 'Where is Cornwall?'

'Brody, show him the map,' said Mrs Dempster.

Brody opened the map and gave it to Aziz.

Aziz looked at the map quickly and carefully. He saw the name 'Helston'. Helston was near Flamingo Park. Then he saw the words 'Flamingo Park' on the map too. Tom and Sheila were not far away.

'Look – here's Penzance on the map,' said Mrs Dempster. 'The Prince is going to arrive tomorrow evening. His father's enemies are planning to kidnap him in Penzance station. But you can help the Prince. You can stop the kidnappers.'

'How can I help him?' asked Aziz.

'You must pretend to *be* the Prince,' replied Mrs Dempster.

'I don't understand,' said Aziz. 'How will that help the Prince, Mrs Dempster?'

'The Prince will come from London by train,' Mrs Dempster said. 'Before it arrives at Penzance, the train stops at a small station. This station is at a place called

Hayle. Look, here's Hayle.'

She pointed at the map and once again Aziz looked at it.

The Prince will get off the train at Hayle,' Mrs Dempster went on. 'You will get on the train and you will pretend to be the Prince.'

'But what will happen then?' asked Aziz.

'When the train arrives at Penzance station, someone will meet you,' said Mrs Dempster. 'This man has been asked to meet Prince Khalifa. But he has never *seen* the Prince. You must pretend to *be* the Prince.'

'You must pretend to be the Prince for as long as possible,' said Brody. 'That will give us time to take the Prince to a safe place. But when the kidnappers know what has happened, they will let you go. They will not hurt you.'

'Will you do that to help the Prince?' asked Mrs Dempster.

'Yes, I'll do that,' said Aziz.

'Wonderful!' said Mrs Dempster. 'You are a brave young man! Why don't you go for a walk now, Aziz? It's a lovely afternoon. But don't go far. It's easy to become lost in the woods.'

Aziz left the house and walked slowly along a path. There were tall trees and thick bushes on each side of the path.

At first, Aziz thought about escaping.

'I'll find the road to Helston,' he said to himself. 'Then I'll go to Flamingo Park.'

But as he walked along the path, the young man thought carefully. Was the Prince really in danger? Perhaps he could help him. Aziz decided to stay with Mrs Dempster and her friends.

When he got back to the house, the kitchen was empty. The map was on the table. Aziz looked at it again.

There was a mark – a cross – by the word 'Hayle'. There was another cross by the words 'Flamingo Park'. Beside the words 'Flamingo Park', was printed 'Tin Mine'. These two words had been underlined in ink.

'What do these marks mean?' Aziz asked himself.

That evening, Aziz sat in the kitchen with Mrs Dempster, Brody and Bill. They watched television.

Early the next morning, Bill drove away in his car. The day passed slowly. At six o'clock in the evening, Mrs Dempster gave Aziz a bag.

'Go to your room and change into these clothes, Aziz,' she said. 'We must leave soon.'

Aziz went into his bedroom. He opened the bag. Inside, he found some clothes. But they were not Western clothes like his own. They were the clothes of an Arab prince. He put them on.

Then Brody, Mrs Dempster and Aziz got into Brody's car, and Brody drove them to Hayle station. On the way, Mrs Dempster gave Aziz a train ticket for the journey to Penzance.

At Hayle station, Mrs Dempster walked onto the platform with Aziz. After a few minutes, a train arrived at the platform. When the train stopped, Mrs Dempster opened a door and pushed Aziz quickly into the train.

'We are going to pay you all your money now,' she said. 'Here it is, in this envelope. And remember, when you get to Penzance, you are Prince Khalifa. Goodbye.'

She put an envelope into the student's hand and slammed the door.

As the train was leaving, Aziz opened the window in the door. He looked back along the platform and he saw something very strange. Bill and Brody were holding a young man. They were holding his arms and they were putting him into a wheelchair. The young man was wearing the clothes of an Arab prince. His clothes were like the clothes which Aziz was wearing.

Aziz sat down on a seat. He opened the envelope. Inside, there was one thousand pounds!

The young student thought about everything that had happened to him. He remembered the small, dirty office in Fenton Street. He thought about Dempster and Brody. How cruel they both looked! And Bill! How tough he looked!

These people had tried to drug Aziz. And Aziz had heard Mrs Dempster talking about a plan. A plan to kidnap someone!

Suddenly, the young man knew the truth. He was not helping these people to save Prince Khalifa. He was helping them to kidnap him! Dempster, Brody and Bill were the kidnappers. And he had taken money from them! He was part of their crime!

Aziz was worried. He *did* want to help Prince Khalifa. What could he do?

Dempster, Brody and Bill were the kidnappers.
And Aziz was part of their crime!

7

Rescue

As soon as the train stopped at Penzance, Aziz got out of it. He looked around. After a moment, a man came up to him.

'I'm Jim Wood,' the man said. 'Are you Prince Khalifa?'

'No! I'm not the Prince. Something terrible has happened,' Aziz began. Then he told the man his story and he showed him the money.

'We must tell the police immediately,' said Aziz.

'Wait a moment,' said Mr Wood. 'We must be very careful. I'm a friend of Prince Khalifa's father. I know the Prince's father very well. He won't want this story to be in the newspapers. Let's sit in my car and think about this problem.'

Jim Wood listened carefully once again to the student's story.

'You noticed something marked on their map,' Jim Wood said to Aziz. 'What was it?'

'There were marks on the map near the words "Flamingo Park" and near the words "Tin Mine",' replied Aziz.

'Can you remember anything else about the map?' Jim Wood asked.

'No, I can't,' replied Aziz. 'But perhaps Flamingo Park is important in the kidnappers' plan. I've got two friends who work at Flamingo Park. They'll help us. Let's go there straightaway.'

Jim Wood started the car and they drove off.

———

It was after ten o'clock when Aziz and Jim Wood arrived at Flamingo Park. It was beginning to get dark. Tom and Sheila were very surprised to see Aziz.

'Aziz! Aziz!' shouted Tom. 'I don't believe it!'

'Why are you dressed in those clothes? asked Sheila.

Aziz introduced Jim Wood and quickly told his friends about the kidnapping of Prince Khalifa.

'Yes! There *was* something strange about that ad,' said Sheila. 'I warned you about it!'

'What did you say about an old tin mine?' asked Tom.

'The mine was marked on the map near Flamingo Park. The words were underlined,' said Aziz.

'Yes, there is an old tin mine near here,' said Tom. 'Sheila and I have looked inside it. But let's go and ask Dave Morris. He's the manager of Flamingo Park. He knows all about the old mine.'

Aziz and Jim Wood hurried with Tom and Sheila to Dave Morris' office. Tom quickly told Dave about the kidnapping of the Prince.

'And the kidnappers had marked the old tin mine on the map,' said Dave.

'Yes,' said Aziz. 'Flamingo Park was marked and so was the tin mine.'

'It's a very old tin mine,' said Dave. 'Many years ago, criminals often hid in there. They often waited there for boats. The boats brought illegal goods from abroad.'

'That's the plan!' said Tom. 'The kidnappers are

keeping the Prince in the mine. And they're waiting for a boat.'

'How can we stop them leaving the country?' asked Jim Wood.

'The entrance to the old mine is near the beach,' said Dave. 'But there's another way into the mine. There are stairs which lead down into the mine, from the top of the cliff.'

'One of you must come with me,' went on Dave. 'We'll climb down the stairs. When the kidnappers hear us, they'll run out onto the beach. Then the rest of you will catch them.'

'I'll go with you,' said Aziz.

'And I'll go with Sheila and Tom,' said Jim Wood. 'We'll go down to the beach.'

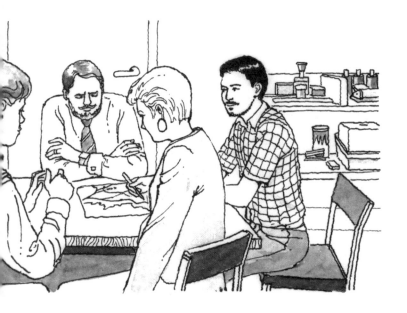

Jim Wood hurried towards the beach with Tom and Sheila.

'Look,' said Tom, as he ran down the path. 'There's a light shining on the water. It's a boat. It's coming to the beach. The kidnappers are going to escape.'

And they ran more quickly.

Dave and Aziz ran to the top of the cliff. Dave was carrying a big torch.

At the top of the cliff, Dave switched on the torch. He shone its light into a large hole in the ground. There were iron stairs leading down into the mine. The old stairs were badly worn and some were broken. Dave climbed down into the hole and Aziz followed him.

Suddenly, there were no more stairs. Dave and Aziz were in a long, dark tunnel. There were many broken rocks on the ground.

After a moment, they heard a noise. Dave switched off the torch and they listened. Someone was shouting in Arabic. Aziz had heard the words before. He had heard them in his dream – 'Help! Help! Get me out!'

'It's Prince Khalifa!' shouted Aziz. 'We've found him.'

Out on the beach, Dempster and Brody were running towards a small boat. Bill was behind them. He was trying to pull the Prince towards the boat.

'Wait for me!' he shouted to Dempster and Brody. But the other two criminals did not stop. In a moment, they had got into the boat.

Bill saw Tom running along the beach towards him.

He let the Prince go, and Bill ran towards the boat. He jumped into it, and the boat turned away from the beach, towards the open sea.

So the three criminals had escaped. But Prince
Khalifa was safe!

Soon, everybody was back in Dave Morris' office. Prince Khalifa told the others about the kidnap.

'Thank you for helping me. My father will be very pleased with all of you,' he said.

Points for Understanding

1

1 All the students at Farraday College liked Aziz, and his teachers were pleased with him. Why?
2 What could people do when they went to Flamingo Park?
3 When the three friends said goodbye, Sheila was worried about Aziz. Why?

2

1 When Aziz went into Flat 7 at 23A Fenton Street, he was surprised. Why?
2 'You will be a companion to a young prince,' Brody told Aziz. What does 'companion' mean here?
3 Why did Aziz decide to take the job?

3

1 Tom and Sheila were hitch-hiking to Cornwall. What does 'hitch-hiking' mean?
2 'The holidaymakers slept in the caravans and tents.' What is a holidaymaker?
3 What is a tin mine?
   Why did Tom want to see one?

4

1 On Friday afternoon, Aziz wanted to talk to Tom and Sheila. Why?
2 Aziz and Bill had a meal at Membury Services. What happened next?
3 Why was Aziz happy when he saw the signpost at the crossroads?

5

1 Aziz poured his coffee into a plant pot. Why?
2 Brody and Dempster were planning to kidnap a prince.
   Why did they need the help of Aziz?
3 Brody and Dempster were going to kidnap Prince Khalifa
   at Hayle.
   Why were they not going to kidnap him at Penzance?

6

1 When Aziz had lunch with Brody, Dempster and Bill, he
   had to pretend to be happy. Why?
2 Aziz decided to stay with Mrs Dempster and her friends.
   Why?
3 In the train, Aziz opened his envelope. Suddenly, he knew
   the truth.
   (a) What was the truth?
   (b) Was Aziz happy when he knew the truth?

7

1 Jim Wood did not want to tell the police about the
   kidnap. Why not?
2 Aziz heard someone on the beach, shouting Arabic words.
   Where had he heard the words before?

Macmillan Heinemann English Language Teaching, Oxford

A division of Macmillan Publishers Limited

Companies and representatives throughout the world

ISBN 0333 74200 1

Heinemann is a registered trademark of Reed Educational & Professional Publishing Limited

Text © John Milne 1987
Design and illustration © Macmillan Publishers Limited 1998
First published 1987 as part of the Focus Reading Series
This edition published 1998

Illustrated by Chris Evans
Typography by Adrian Hodgkins
Designed by Sue Vaudin
Cover by Marketplace Design
Typeset in 11½/14½pt Goudy
Printed and bound in Great Britain
by Fineprint (Services) Ltd, Oxford

98 99 00 01 02 10 9 8 7 6 5 4 3 2 1